HighTide Festival Theatre present

THE GIRL'S GUIDE TO SAVING THE WORLD

A world premiere by Elinor Cook

This production of *The Girl's Guide to Saving the World* was first produced as part of the 2014 HighTide Festival, Halesworth, Suffolk on 11 April 2014

Production supported by

Split Infinitive Trust

THE GIRL'S GUIDE TO SAVING THE WORLD

A world premiere by Elinor Cook
A HighTide Festival Theatre Production

JANE	Jade Williams
BELLA/WOMAN	Georgina Strawson
TOBY/MAN/BOY	Ben Lambert
Director	Amelia Sears
Set and Costume Designer	Jamie Vartan
Lighting Designer	Malcolm Rippeth
Sound Designer	Elena Peña
Casting Director	Hayley Kaimakliotis CDG
Production Manager	Cath Bates
Technical Manager	James Hirst
Stage Manager	Hannah Boustred

The Producers wish to thank:
Clare Couchman, Fay Davies, Harriet Devine, Amy Hodge,
Aneta Ivanova

Cast

Jade Williams (*Jane*)
Theatre includes: *Moon Tiger* (Theatre Royal Bath); *Cake and Congo* (Theatre503); *Sons Without Fathers* from Chekhov's *Platonov*, *Palace of the End* (Arcola); *In Basildon* (Royal Court); *Doctor Faustus*, *The God of Soho*, *Henry IV Part I & II*, *Bedlam*, *As You Like It*, *A New World* (Shakespeare's Globe); *Romeo and Juliet* (Globe/UK tour); *Shraddha*, *Piranha Heights* (Soho); *Chatroom/Citizenship* (National/Hong Kong Arts Festival); *Market Boy* (National Theatre); *I Like Mine with a Kiss* (Bush); *The Little Prince* (Hampstead); *'Low Dat* (Birmingham Rep).

Television includes: *DCI Banks*, *William and Mary*, *Bad Girls*, *Serious and Organised*, *The Bill*, *Lloyd & Hill* (ITV); *Shakespeare Uncovered* (PBS/Sky Arts); *Holby City*, *EastEnders*, *Judge John Deed*, *The Canterbury Tales*, *Being April*, *Doctors*, *Casualty*, *Plotlands*, *Blackhearts in Battersea* (BBC); *Mile High* (Sky).

Film includes: *Anne Frank* (Emmy Award-winning drama for ABC); *Life and Lyrics* (Universal); *Hush Your Mouth* (Greenwich Films).

Radio includes: *The Gate of Angels*, *Marnie*, *Arcadia*, *Five Wedding Dresses – The Rescue*, *Needle*, *The Chronicles of Narnia*, *Secrets*, *The Third Trial*, *The Mother of…*, *The Family Man*, *The Birds*, *What Is She Doing Here?*, *The Day the Planes Came*, *Westway*.

Georgina Strawson (*Bella/Woman*)
Theatre includes: *Middlemarch Trilogy* (Orange Tree); *True Blue* (Theatre503); *The Winslow Boy*, *Macbeth* (Bolton, Octagon); *Swifter, Higher, Stronger* (Roundhouse); *Taking Steps* (Old Laundry Theatre).

Television includes: *Phoneshop* (Channel 4); *Lewis* (ITV); *The Crinklewood Greats* (BBC 4).

Ben Lambert (*Toby/Man/Boy*)
Theatre includes: *Middlemarch Trilogy* (Orange Tree); *Boiling Frogs*, *Revenger's Tragedy* (Southwark Playhouse); *Hamlet*, *Round One* (The Factory); *The History Boys* (West Yorkshire Playhouse/No1 tour); *Chimps* (Ipswich New Wolsey); *Romeo and Juliet* (Shakespeare's Globe); *A Trip to Scarborough*, *Touch Wood*, *Forget Me Not Lane* (Stephen Joseph); *French Without Tears* (ETT); *Gates of Gold* (Trafalgar Studios); *Arrows* (Greenwich Playhouse); *Tamburlaine* (Bristol Old Vic); *Macbeth* (Almeida).

Television includes: *DCI Banks* (BBC); *C.S. Lewis & the Spirit of Narnia* (HBO).

Film includes: *Outpost: Rise of the Spetsnaz* (Black Camel); *Zero Dark Thirty* (Annapurna Films); *Vampyre Nation* (SyFy Channel); *Jamaica Me Crazy* (Rumor Productions); *Song of Songs*; *The Open Door*.

Creatives

Elinor Cook (Writer)
Theatre includes: *The Girl's Guide to Saving The World* (HighTide Festival); *this is where we got to when you came in* (non zero one/ Bush). Elinor won the 2014 George Devine Award.

Hayley Kaimakliotis CDG (Casting)
For HighTide: *Incognito* (and nabokov/Live Theatre, Newcastle/ North Wall/Bush); *Stuart: A Life Backwards* (and Edinburgh/Watford Palace Theatre/Sheffield Theatres); *Neighbors* (and Nuffield, Southampton); *Mudlarks* (and Bush Theatre/Theatre503). Other theatre includes: *The Tempest Suitcase Shakespeare* (RSC); *Pitcairn* workshop (Out of Joint/RSC); *The Only True History of Lizzie Finn* (Southwark Playhouse); *Firewatchers* (Old Red Lion); *Amphibians* (Bridewell); *A Midsummer Night's Dream* (Wirksworth Festival/Riverside Studios). As Casting Director for the Finborough: *Facts*, the award-winning *Accolade* and *Foxfinder*, *Don Juan*, *Crush*, *Rigor Mortis*, *Fanta Orange*, *Drama at Inish*, *Me and Juliet*, *Miss Lilly Gets Boned*, *The Northerners* and numerous *Vibrant* seasons.

Casting assistant includes: *Shakespeare in Love* (Noël Coward Theatre); *Very Few Fish*, *Watson and Oliver* Series 2, *Autumn Leaves*, *Doctors*, *Casualty*, *Holby City*, *EastEnders* (BBC); *Troilus and Cressida*, *Forests*, *The Merry Wives of Windsor*, *The Mouse and His Child*, *Boris Godunov*, *Life of Galileo*, *As You Like It*, *All's Well That Ends Well* and *Hamlet* (RSC). Hayley is a probationary member of the CDG.

Elena Peña (Sound Designer)
Theatre includes: *Not Now Bernard* (Unicorn); *Macbeth: Blood Will Have Blood* (China Plate); *Pim & Theo* (NIE/Odsherred Teater, Denmark); *The Planet and Stuff* (Polka); *Hackford Road* (Art Angel); *A High Street Odyssey* (Inspector Sands); *Flashes* (Young Vic); *Arabian Nights* (Tricycle); *Mass Observation* (Almeida); *Brimstone and Treacle* (Arcola); *Twelve Years* (BBC Radio 4 Drama); *Gambling* (Soho); *The 13 Midnight Challenges of Angelus Diablo* (RSC); *Quimeras* (Sadler's Wells/Edinburgh International Festival); *Unbroken* (Gate); *Plasticine* (Southwark Playhouse); *Under Milk Wood* (Northampton Theatre Royal).

Malcolm Rippeth (Lighting Designer)
Theatre includes: *The Empress* (RSC); *The Promise* (Donmar Warehouse); *Spur of the Moment* (Royal Court); *Spring Awakening* (Headlong); *Stones in his Pockets* (Tricycle); *The Night Before Christmas* (Soho); *The Dead* (Abbey, Dublin); *The Birthday Party* (Manchester Royal Exchange); *London* (Paines Plough); *The Threepenny Opera* (Graeae); *West Side Story* (Sage Gateshead);

Refugee Boy (West Yorkshire Playhouse); *His Dark Materials* (Birmingham Rep); *Moon Tiger* (Theatre Royal Bath); *Calendar Girls* (West End/Australia/Canada); *HMS Pinafore* (Guthrie Theater, Minneapolis); *Copenhagen* (Royal Lyceum Edinburgh); *Le Nozze di Figaro* (Garsington Opera); *Seven Deadly Sins* (WNO); *Rapunzel* (balletLORENT). Malcolm is an Associate Artist of Kneehigh Theatre, productions including *Tristan & Yseult, The Wild Bride, The Red Shoes, Wah! Wah! Girls, The Umbrellas of Cherbourg* and *Brief Encounter* (whatsonstage.com and OBIE Awards).

Amelia Sears (Director)
Theatre includes: *Home* by David Storey, *Brimstone and Treacle* by Dennis Potter (Arcola); *Flashes* (parallel project) by Silva Semerciyan (Young Vic, Maria); *Swifter, Higher, Stronger* by Abi Zakarian (Roundhouse); *The Last 5 Years* by Jason Robert Brown (Duchess).

As Associate Director includes: *Ghosts* (Duchess); *Twelfth Night* (Wyndham's); *...Some Trace of Her, The Year of Magical Thinking, Statement of Regret* (National Theatre). Awards: recipient of the Bulldog Princep Bursary at the National Theatre Studio 2008.

Jamie Vartan (Designer)
Theatre includes: three years as designer and artist-in-residence with the David Glass Ensemble on *The Lost Child Trilogy*, including residencies in Vietnam, Indonesia, China, the Philippines and Colombia; *The Last Yankee* (The Print Room); *Mass Observation* (Almeida); *Vertigo, Breaking the Silence* (Nottingham Playhouse); *Mrs Warren's Profession, The Playboy of the Western World* (National Theatre of Ireland/Abbey/Peacock Theatres); *Misterman* starring Cillian Murphy (St Anne's Warehouse, National Theatre Lyttleton – Irish Times Best Set Design Award 2012, Evening Standard Best Set Design Nomination).

Current work includes *Khandan* (Birmingham Rep/Royal Court) and a new play by Enda Walsh, *Ballyturk* (Galway Arts Festival 2014 and National Theatre Lyttleton).

Opera includes: Productions at Malmö Opera; Salzburg Festspielhaus; Opéra de Marseille, Teatro São Carlos, Lisbon; La Scala, Milan; Teatro Lirico di Cagliari; Teatro di San Carlo, Naples; Teatro Comunale, Florence; Teatro Farnese, Parma; the Royal Opera House and Scottish Opera. His design for *A Village Romeo and Juliet* (Wexford Opera), won the Irish Times Best Set Design Award 2013. Jamie has worked extensively as a designer in theatre, opera and dance in the UK and Europe and has represented the UK at Prague Quadrennials in 1999, 2007 and 2011.

HighTide Festival Theatre

Makers of New Theatre

"One of the little gems of the artistic calendar in Britain" The Telegraph

"Famous for championing emerging playwrights and contemporary theatre" Daily Mail

HighTide Festival Theatre is one of the UK's leading producers of new plays, and the only professional theatre focused on the production of new playwrights. Currently we read and consider around 1000 scripts a year from around the world, from which we then work with 100 playwrights on a range of development opportunities, from workshops to full productions. Every play that we receive is read by our Artistic Director and Associates.

Under Steven Atkinson, co-founding Artistic Director, we have premièred major productions by playwrights including Ella Hickson, Frances Ya-Chu Cowhig, Nick Payne, Adam Brace, Beth Steel, Laura Poliakoff, Luke Barnes, Vickie Donoghue, Lydia Adetunji, Jack Thorne and Joel Horwood. We produce several productions a year in our annual Suffolk festival and on tour.

In seven years we have staged over fifty productions, producing new work with some of the world's leading theatres in London (including the National Theatre, Bush Theatre, Old Vic Theatre and Soho Theatre), regionally (including Sheffield Theatres, Watford Palace and Theatre Royal Bath) and internationally (In New York 59E59 and the Public Theater, and in Australia the National Play Festival).

Lansons host our administrative offices in-kind within their Clerkenwell offices. This innovative partnership between a business and charity has won five Corporate Engagement Awards, a Social Impact Award, an Arts & Business award nomination, and has been profiled by the Guardian and the Evening Standard.

HighTide Festival Theatre is a National Portfolio Organisation of Arts Council England.

HT
2014

Our 2014 Season will commence with the transfer of Chris Dunkley's *Smallholding* to Soho Theatre.

Nadezhda Tolokonnikova's *Pussy Riot: Letters and Writings* will be performed at the Southbank Centre as part of the 2014 Women of the World Festival.

Then the eighth HighTide Festival will take place in Halesworth, Suffolk from April 10 to 19. The festival will give Elinor Cook and Harry Melling their professional debuts, Nick Payne returns to the festival for the first time since 2008, and we will produce the European premiere of Dan LeFranc's award-winning *The Big Meal* directed by Michael Boyd.

The Big Meal will premiere at the Ustinov Studio before transferring to the HighTide Festival in a co-production with Bath Theatre Royal Productions.

Nick Payne's *Incognito* will transfer to Live Theatre Newcastle, the North Wall Oxford and the Bush Theatre in a co-production with nabokov and Live Theatre.

Harry Melling's *peddling* will transfer to 59E59, New York, as part of Brits Off-Broadway.

For full details please visit www.hightide.org.uk

Image: **Boys** by Ella Hickson (HighTide 2012)
Photographer: Bill Knight

HighTide Festival Theatre
24a St John Street, London, EC1M 4AY
0207 566 9765 : hello@hightide.org.uk : www.hightide.org.uk

HighTide Company
Artistic Director – Steven Atkinson
Executive Director – Holly Kendrick
Producer – Francesca Clark
Marketing and Development Officer – Freddie Porter
Literary Associate – Stephanie Street

Festival Company
Production Manager – Cath Bates
Technical Manager – James Hirst
Company and General Manager – Jennifer Willey
Head of Lighting – Barry Abbotts
Head of Sound – Mark Cunningham
Master Carpenter – David Larking
Costume Supervisor and Wardrobe – Stephen Frosdick
Venue Stage Managers and Festival Technicians – Gabriel Bartlett, Richard Bell, Marc Gough,
Suzie Inglis, Andrew McCabe and Keith Zukowski,

Marketing and Press
Marketing Consultant – JHI – 020 7420 7730
Marketing Design – Chris Perkin
Press – Dee McCourt and Giles Cooper for Borkowski Arts & Ents– 020 3176 2700

Artistic Associates
Tom Attenborough, Justin Audibert, Richard Beecham, Ella Hickson, Paul Jellis, Blanche
MacIntyre, Prasanna Puwanarajah, Chris Thorpe, Will Wrightson

Escalator Playwrights-on-Attachment
Georgia Christou, Vickie Donoghue, Marcelo Dos Santos, Louise Gooding, Daniel Kanaber,
Nessah Muthy, Vinay Patel, Sophie Stanton

In 2013-14 HighTide has collaborated with:
Sheffield Theatres; Watford Palace Theatre; Underbelly; Soho Theatre; Theatre Royal Bath;
nabakov; Live Theatre, Newcastle; North Wall, Oxford; 59E59, New York City; IdeasTap; Bush
Theatre; Nuffield, Southampton; Royal & Derngate, Northampton.

Board
Steven Atkinson, Amy Bird, Peter Clayton, Sue Emmas, Emma Freud OBE, Nick Giles, Diana
Hiddleston, Mark Lacey, Criona Palmer, Clare Parsons, Tali Pelman, Mark Rhodes, Dallas Smith,
Graham White, Peter Wilson MBE (Chair)

Advisory Council
Jack Bradley, Robert Fox, Thelma Holt CBE, Mel Kenyon, Tom Morris, Roger Wingate

Patrons
Sinead Cusack, Stephen Daldry CBE, Sir Richard Eyre CBE, Sally Greene OBE, Sir David Hare,
Sir Nicholas Hytner, Sam Mendes CBE, Juliet Stevenson CBE

The Garrick Charitable Trust, The Scarfe Charitable Trust and Split Infinitive Trust

Charitable Support

HighTide is a registered charity (1124477) and we are grateful to the many organisations and individuals who support our work, enabling us to keep our ticket prices low and accessible to many different audiences around the world.

> *'There are very talented young playwrights working in the UK, and if they are lucky they will find their way to the HighTide Festival Theatre season in Suffolk. I hope you will join me in supporting this remarkable and modest organisation. With your help HighTide can play an even more major role in promoting the best of new writing in the UK.'* **Lady Susie Sainsbury**

HighTide Festival Theatre is a National Portfolio Organisation of Arts Council England.

Major Supporters
Arts Council England, Lansons, Old Possums Practical Trust, Suffolk County Council, The Backstage Trust, The Garfield Weston Foundation, IdeasTap.

Corporate Supporters
AEM International, John Clayton and Bishops Printers, Jo Hutchison International, CMS Cameron McKenna.

Individual Supporters
Diana Hiddleston, Clare Parsons and Tony Langham, Criona Palmer and Tony Mackintosh, Albert and Marjorie Scardino, Peter Wilson MBE.

Trusts and Foundations
Chivers Trust, Fidelio Charitable Trust, The Garrick Charitable Trust, The Golsoncott Foundation, The Leche Trust, The Mackintosh Foundation, The Harold Hyam Wingate Foundation, Margaret Guido's Charitable Trust, The Parham Trust, Royal Victoria Hall Foundation, Scarfe Charitable Trust, Split Infinitive Trust.

With thanks to Shoreditch Town Hall and all our Friends of the Festival and Host Families.

How to Support HighTide
If you are interested in supporting our work, please contact Freddie Porter on 0207 566 9765 or email freddie@hightide.org.uk

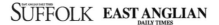

Artistic Development

Send us your Play

At HighTide we pride ourselves on discovering new playwrights and giving their play a world-class production. If you are a playwright looking for your big break, then we want to read the best unproduced play you have.

We accept scripts from around the world via our partner website IdeasTap. Scripts are read by our Artistic Director and Artistic Associates. Of the 1000 scripts we receive annually, 100 writers are then invited to work with the company through workshops, readings, and full productions.

Our submission window is open twice a year. To submit a play please visit: **www.ideastap.com/Partners/hightide**

Escalator Plays

Escalator Plays is a talent development initiative that is supported by Arts Council England South East.

The scheme is designed to support early career playwrights from the South East of England, and those wanting to work in the region to develop their work and showcase their work at partner theatres, who have included Eastern Angles, Mercury Theatre Colchester and Watford Palace Theatre.

As part of a writers' group, six writers each year will be offered a bespoke package of development which is a means to grow their own writing and capacity to see that work produced. Escalator Plays aims to improve the quality of each writer's work and connect each of the group to the wider theatre industry within the region. This development will include access to one-on-one sessions, workshops, time with creatives and other writers and may lead to work being shared or fully produced in the future.

Applications for the 2015 Escalator Plays intake open in autumn 2014. For more information see **www.hightide.org.uk/escalator_plays**

For more information about working with HighTide please contact Stephanie Street, Literary Associate: stephanie@hightide.org.uk

THE GIRL'S GUIDE TO SAVING THE WORLD

Elinor Cook

For Anna Barnes,
who unintentionally gave me the title

Characters

JANE
BELLA
MAN
TOBY
BOY
WOMAN

They are all approximately twenty-nine years old

Acknowledgements

I'd like to thank my agent Fay Davies; Steven Atkinson for
seeing something in the play in its earliest incarnation; Alice,
Katie, Chloe and Livi who inspired so much of the material;
Leo Butler and the Royal Court Supergroup 2012; Jennifer
Strawson; Guy and my family for their support; and especially
Amelia Sears.

E.C.

*This text went to press before the end of rehearsals and so may
differ slightly from the play as performed.*

#

JANE *and* BELLA.

A pregnancy test.

JANE	How long is it again?
BELLA	Two minutes.
JANE	OK.

Pause.

I think I've got some of your pee on my thumb.

BELLA	So cry about it.
JANE	Yup. Fair point.

Pause.

Oh shit a line's come up.
Bella.
A blue line.

BELLA	What?
JANE	Oh no wait. Wait. That always happens.
BELLA	What the actual fuck?
JANE	That just means it's working.
BELLA	Check the packet. Check the packet, Jane.
JANE	Uh – Uh yes, look. It's *two* blue lines. Two blue lines you've got to worry about.

BELLA	Jesus. Don't do that.
JANE	I'm sorry.
BELLA	You've got to keep your head, Jane.
JANE	I am.
BELLA	You can't panic.
JANE	I won't.
BELLA	Fuck.
JANE	Sorry.
BELLA	How long has it been?
JANE	Not yet.
BELLA	Jesus.
JANE	Why am I the one holding this?
BELLA	I can't sit there and watch my fate get sealed in my own hand.
JANE	Can I put it on the floor?
BELLA	What? Why?
JANE	I don't know. It's a lot of pressure. Like a tiny bomb or something.
BELLA	You can't put it on the floor.
JANE	Why not?
BELLA	A random chemical. Might interfere. Cause some sort of reaction.
JANE	I don't think it will –
BELLA	Don't put it on the floor.
JANE	OK.

Beat.

BELLA   This is bullshit.
             Isn't this bullshit?

JANE   Absolute bullshit.

BELLA   Fucking tosser.
             Am I right?

JANE   Of course.
             Absolute prick.

BELLA   'I don't LIKE condoms.
             They're too SMALL.
             It ruins the MOMENT.'

JANE   Fucking arsehole.

BELLA   I'd like to see him.
             Wedged in a bathroom.
             Peeing on a stick.

JANE   He doesn't have to.

BELLA   How fucked up is that?

JANE   It's totally fucked up.

BELLA   'I've never *needed* to have an STD test.
             I'm as pure as the fresh-driven SNOW.'

JANE   Fuckstick.

BELLA   Prickarse.

JANE   Still.
             You let him.

BELLA   Pardon?

JANE   I'm just saying.
             You could have insisted.
             Right?

BELLA   Whose side are you on?

JANE   Yours.

BELLA   I'm saying it's an embedded societal attitude.

JANE   You've said that a few times.
          But still –

BELLA   Don't sheath the penis!
          You might scare it!
          Let it flourish in all its quivering, unfettered glory!

JANE   Well.

          Beat.

BELLA   OK you're right.
          I'm a dick.

JANE   No.

BELLA   I'm just as much to blame.

JANE   No.

BELLA   I need to fucking get a grip.

JANE   Of course not.

BELLA   Stop being such a slut.

JANE   You're not a slut.

BELLA   Yeah right.

JANE   Yeah but.
          So what?
          So what if you're a bit slutty?

BELLA   Well.
          OK.
          Exactly.

JANE   Why should you have to apologise for that?

BELLA   I'm not apologising.

JANE   Too right.

BELLA   Men don't have to apologise.

JANE   Nope.

BELLA   Time yet?

JANE   Nope.

BELLA   Men are celebrated for their bountiful sexual
            encounters.

JANE   Not long.

BELLA   Whereas me –
            ME.
            How dare I derive pleasure from casual carnal
            liaisons?
            (Don't look at it yet.
            Don't.)

JANE   OK.

BELLA   Instead of –
            You know –
            How dare I not be posting millions and millions of
            pictures of my *wedding* on Facebook?

JANE   Yep.

BELLA   I should just be –
            You know.
            Sitting quietly, reading a magazine, learning why
            Nicole is looking so SAD and GAUNT.

JANE   Yep.
            Sure.

BELLA   ABANDONED yet again for SVELTE
            TEENAGER.

JANE   Or looking RELAXED on holiday with
            GORGEOUS rounded BELLY.

BELLA   Next to a picture of her dipping a carrot baton –

JANE   In a teeny-tiny dollop of mayonnaise.

BELLA   Because I'm a girl!

JANE   A GIRL!
            I love cupcakes!

BELLA   I'm really ditsy and clumsy but it's totally adorable!

JANE   I'm so CUTE!

sitting on the toilet?

BELLA	I totally aspire to be a prepubescent creature in an American Apparel campaign.
JANE	Wearing a vest.
BELLA	Woozy from the Rohypnol.
JANE	Glassy-eyed and drooling.
BELLA	Wobbly on my frail little Bambi legs.
JANE	My dewy, milky skin dimpling in the cold.
BELLA	Oh please Mr Photographer – Please can I just fellate you while you tell me all about your awesome career hanging out with all the MODELS!
JANE	I really wanna hear ALL ABOUT IT.
BELLA	You've had such an AMAZING LIFE.
JANE	Oh and please Magazine Editor Lady – Please exploit my flawless youth and touchable body.
BELLA	Please let me wear all these really expensive, see-through clothes in a vague desert location.
JANE	Please love me for having famous parents.
BELLA	Also can you please sign off all your columns with a little kiss?
JANE	Cos you *know* me. You *understand* me.
BELLA	Oh and please can you tell me how much all female celebrities WEIGH so that I can compare myself?
JANE	Can you maybe give me some tips on how I can stop my man from leaving me?
BELLA	Yeah can you give me some HOT sex tips please? I really need them.
JANE	Please can you give me an insight into what men find sexy? Cos I just don't hear about that kind of thing enough.

BELLA   'IT WON'T BE WHAT YOU THINK!!!!'

JANE   Take an ice cube –

BELLA   Wear a blindfold –

JANE   Some pink fluffy handcuffs –

BELLA   Light bondage –

JANE   Dominatrix –

BELLA   Stilettos –

JANE   Sensual massage –

BELLA   Chocolate body paint –

JANE   Hum gently on his penis.

BELLA   Worship the penis.

JANE   Bow down before the penis and GIVE THANKS.

            Pause.

BELLA   We should like –
            Tackle this shit –
            This fucking pernicious, evil shit –
            Tackle it head-on.

JANE   Yeah!
            Obviously!

BELLA   I'm being serious.

JANE   OK.
            Really?

BELLA   The internet.
            A blog?

JANE   OK.

BELLA   Become all-pervasive.
            Un-ignorable.

JANE   Everywhere.

BELLA   We can have –
            Ironic pictures.

JANE   Yes.
          Yes –

BELLA   A scathing editorial tone.

JANE   That's also warm and engaging.

BELLA   Articulate and angry.

JANE   A torrent of rage.

BELLA   But also somewhere to turn.

JANE   If you're lost.

BELLA   Confused.

JANE   If you don't know who the hell you are.

BELLA   Cos why the hell would you know?

JANE   Exactly.
          There's no one to guide you.

BELLA   All these women.
          Feeling like failures.

JANE   Adrift in a sea of failure.

BELLA   Feeling afraid to speak out.

JANE   Endlessly nice.
          Pathologically apologetic.

BELLA   Fuck niceness.
          Fuck apology.

JANE   Yes!

BELLA   We'll do it.
          You and me.
          Together.

JANE   YES.

BELLA   YES.

          Pause.

JANE   Time's up.

BELLA   Jane.

JANE   What?

BELLA   Just –
Wait for a moment.

Pause.

Let's just –
Contemplate.
What it might mean.
That little urine-soaked stick.

Pause.

Do you want kids?

JANE   God.
Dunno.

BELLA   Yeah.

Pause.

If I am –

JANE   You won't be.

BELLA   Either it's –
Zip.

JANE   Yup.

BELLA   Or it's –
It's being on the Tube, with a buggy, getting the wheels caught in a spiral staircase and everyone glaring at you while you sweat through your sick-covered T-shirt.

JANE   Yes.

BELLA   It's an endless parade of uneaten banana sandwiches, the mulch squelching under your fingernails, in your hair, caught in your nostrils.

JANE   Yes.

BELLA   It's watching yourself disappear.
It's –

Being hollowed out with love for something that
you can't dare to hope will always love you back…

Pause.

JANE   You'd be a good mother.

BELLA   Pah.

JANE   You would be.

BELLA   What does that even mean?

JANE   It means –
          Well –

BELLA   I'd be a terrible mother.
          Terrible.

          Pause.

          Maybe this is what I want more than anything.

JANE   Is it?

BELLA   That's scary.

          Pause.

          We never used to be scared of anything.

JANE   I know.

BELLA   Remember when we used to play chicken on the
          train tracks by the river?

JANE   God.

BELLA   The way the tracks would start humming –

JANE   Yeah –

BELLA   Just gently –

JANE   Shit.

BELLA   You'd think you were gonna pee yourself.

JANE   I did once.

BELLA   Laughing hysterically even though it was
          completely the opposite of funny.

JANE   The racket the train made as it got closer.

BELLA   Like a monster.

JANE   Fuck it was scary.

BELLA   Always wondering –
           What if I don't make it?
           What if I can't?

JANE   Yes!

BELLA   That was the thrill.

JANE   It was.

BELLA   That was the point.

JANE   Exactly.

           Pause.

BELLA   Why did we stop?

JANE   My mum found out.

BELLA   Your mum is scary.

JANE   I know.

BELLA   Even I'm scared of your mum.

JANE   Everyone's scared of her.

           Beat.

BELLA   OK.

           Beat.

           If I'm not.
           Then.
           That's what we have to do.
           Both of us.

JANE   OK.

BELLA   No more talk.
           Just –
           Action.

JANE   OK.

BELLA   We're going to take down each and every one of
          these harpies.
          With just the power of our razor-sharp tongues.

JANE   Yes.

BELLA   Promise?

JANE   Promise.

BELLA   Don't let me talk myself out of it.

JANE   No.

BELLA   Seriously Jane.
          Don't.

JANE   I promise.

          Pause.

          OK.
          OK you're not pregnant.

          Pause.

BELLA   OK.

          Pause.

          So this is it.
          We're going to do it.

JANE   We are.
          We are?

BELLA   We are.

          Pause.

          They look at each other.

          They nearly laugh.

          Then they steel themselves.

          Shake.

          They shake hands.

#

JANE *and* MAN.

A bus stop.

It's dark.

MAN   Hey?

JANE *is silent.*

Hey.

JANE *is silent.*

I know you don't I?

JANE *is silent.*

Excuse me?
I'm talking to you.
EXCUSE me.

JANE *is silent.*

Oh I get it.
You think that just cos I'm TALKING to you –
I want to RAPE you.

JANE *is silent.*

Well I've got news for you.
You –
Are flattering yourself.

JANE *is silent.*

Do you want to know why?

JANE *is silent.*

Because I like women to be warm.
Compliant.
Friendly.
Kind.
Expansive.
Sheltering.
Maternal.

Nurturing.
Quiet.
Appealingly giggly.

JANE *is silent.*

I like them to intuit my every need.
I like them to let me believe all the thoughts
they've had are my thoughts.
I like them to want me when I want them but not
at any other time.
I like them to be sympathetic when I'm tired,
when I'm grumpy, when my blood sugar is
critically low.

But I also want you to guide me.
It's your job to steer me, to awaken the best in me,
to tease out every facet of my potential.
You can do this via the amazing skills and gifts
that are peculiar to women alone.
The power of manipulation.
Of silky, subtle flattery.
The gift of double-talk, of reverse psychology.
I admire all of those things.
Those gifts that wile and weaken a man.

JANE *is silent.*

So don't sit there and think.
Smugly.
That I don't understand you.
That I don't admire and respect you.
Because I do.
Women.
You make me weak.
With your eyes.
Your smiles.
Your legs.

JANE *stands up.*

Oh don't need the bus any more do you?
How peculiar.
What a strange coincidence.

JANE *begins to move away.*

Well now I'm upset.
You've hurt my feelings.
Do you understand?
Hey.
HEY.

The sound of JANE*'s breathing.*

#

TOBY *and* JANE.

Kitchen.

TOBY	Are you alright?
JANE	What?
TOBY	What's up?
JANE	Oh. Just. Some guy. At the bus stop.
TOBY	What? What guy?
JANE	It was nothing.
TOBY	What did he do?
JANE	Honestly. He was just – Saying stuff.
TOBY	What kind of stuff?
JANE	It doesn't matter.
TOBY	Yes it does.
JANE	I just want to –

TOBY   Jane?

JANE   Forget about it.

TOBY   What did he say to you?

JANE   Just you know –
         The usual.

TOBY   Where is he?

JANE   Oh.
         Long gone.
         Somewhere.

TOBY   Do you want me to find him?

JANE   No.

TOBY   Do you want me to go and –
         And put cyanide in his water supply?

JANE   Uh.
         Yeah OK.

TOBY   OK.
         Consider it done.

         Pause.

JANE   Do you think –
         Deep down –
         That all men secretly hate women?

TOBY   Of course not.
         Hey.
         Come here.

JANE   Am I meant to feel afraid?
         Constantly?
         Is that how I'm supposed to feel?

TOBY   He's a fucktard.
         Don't listen to him.
         You're safe.

         Hug.

         They sink into it.

         There's curry.

JANE   Seriously?

TOBY   Yep.

JANE   I love you.

TOBY   Fish curry.

JANE   I love you for ever.

TOBY   Wilf ate quite a lot of the fish though.

JANE   You're not supposed to give him fish.
            He's only meant to be on the dry food.

TOBY   He's refusing to eat it.

JANE   Still?

TOBY   Yeah.

JANE   Weren't we going to take him to the vet's?

TOBY   I will.
            Next week.

            Pause.

            How's Bella?

JANE   Good.

            Beat.

            We have a plan.

TOBY   Do you?

JANE   A project.

TOBY   That's exciting.

            Beat.

JANE   We're going to –

TOBY   I've got news too.

JANE   Oh.
            Really?

TOBY   Mm.

JANE   What?

        Beat.

TOBY   I quit.

        Beat.

        Today.
        I handed in my notice.

JANE   You quit?
        Your job?

TOBY   I did.

        Pause.

JANE   But –
        But you're a teacher –

TOBY   Was a teacher.

JANE   Teachers are –
        Essential and wonderful and worthy and –

TOBY   Not necessarily, Jane.
        I'm sorry.

        Pause.

JANE   Well –
        Well I didn't realise you weren't enjoying –

TOBY   It's not that.

JANE   Oh.

TOBY   It's –
        Look it's the never-ending battle against –
        Futility.

JANE   Right.

TOBY   I mean.
        Trying to get these kids interested in Literature.
        It's like –
        Like –
        What's the point?

JANE   I –
            I thought that *was* the point.
            The challenge.

TOBY   They don't care.

JANE   Isn't that a bit of a sweeping statement?

TOBY   They –
            They're indifferent.
            I mean I stand there, in front of them –
            With so much passion, so much intent.
            And it just –
            Plummets –
            Into a black hole.

JANE   But you –
            You can't just give up.
            Just like that.

TOBY   They mock it.
            I think that's the most difficult thing to take.
            The fact that they just –
            Mock.

JANE   There must be *one*.
            One shining beacon of hope you can get all
            Dangerous Minds about?

TOBY   That's an illusion.

JANE   Oh.

TOBY   Yeah, sure, you go in full of idealism, *arrogance*.
            You're going to be the one who changes things!
            Inspires!

JANE   Well.
            Yes.

TOBY   But the reality is –
            I mean it's –
            You have no idea, Jane.

JANE   You –
            You never said.

TOBY   Well I'm saying it now.

JANE   Well yes.
          After the event.

          Pause.

TOBY   The point is.
          Look.
          I'm just going to take some time to –
          Figure it out.

JANE   OK.
          Well.
          If that's what you want.

TOBY   It is what I want.

JANE   I think it's a shame but –

TOBY   I'm going to help Pete with his painting and
          decorating stuff.

JANE   Oh.

TOBY   For the time being.

JANE   Right.

TOBY   We're going to start with this place.

JANE   Here?

TOBY   Yeah.

JANE   Right.
          Who's going to be –
          Paying for that.

          Beat.

TOBY   Mum's always saying it's a shame it's so dingy.

JANE   Your mum's paying you to redecorate our flat?

TOBY   Early Christmas present.

JANE   To who?

TOBY   You.

JANE Oh.

   Silence.

TOBY I know it's a big change.

JANE Well no but.
   Yes.
   Obviously I want you to be happy.

TOBY I know it's not exactly conventional.

JANE No.
   No.

TOBY But I think it's going to be such a positive thing
   for me.
   For us.
   In the long run.

JANE Right.
   OK.
   Yes.
   A change of tack.
   That's OK.
   That's great.

TOBY You think?

JANE I mean –
   I mean it's not like you're going to be one of those
   Jeremy Kyle losers.
   Watching *Cash in the Attic*.
   Is it?

TOBY No.

JANE You'll be planning and focusing and, and –
   Making spider diagrams and stuff.
   In the library.

TOBY Right.

JANE Mind-maps.

TOBY Yeah.

JANE   Thinking creatively.
        Laterally.

TOBY   Sure.

JANE   You can be one of those cool, notebook-in-coffee-
        shop people.
        I mean.
        Everyone wants to be that guy!

        Pause.

        Don't they?

TOBY   Look I should probably phone Mum.

JANE   OK.
        Good idea.

        Beat.

        And after you get off the phone.
        I might be like, completely naked.

TOBY   Ah.
        Yeah?

JANE   Just, like, waiting for you.

TOBY   Uh-huh.

JANE   Yep.

TOBY   Right.

JANE   Put that in your pipe and –

        Beat.

TOBY   Sure um.
        Will do.

JANE   Cool.

TOBY   Yup.

JANE   That's right.

        They look at each other.

        OK so.
        Good luck.

TOBY   Thanks.
              Thanks yeah.

              TOBY *exits*.

              JANE *is alone*.

              Slowly she removes her tights.

              Looks at them.

              Puts them back on.

\#

BELLA, JANE, BOY.

A party.

It's loud.

BELLA   Can you zip me up?

JANE   What?

BELLA   My dress.

JANE   Oh.
              So that's what you've been up to.

BELLA   Was I ages?

JANE   A bit.

BELLA   Where's Toby?

JANE   Went home.

BELLA   He needs to slow down.

JANE   Huh?

BELLA   I said he needs to *slow down*.

JANE   Oh.
              Ha.

BELLA   You see that guy?

JANE   Which one?

BELLA   The one in the corner.
          On his own.
          Looks like a lost nineteenth-century poet.
          Or a Russian prince.

JANE   Is he the one you just – ?

BELLA   Durr, no!

JANE   Oh.

BELLA   But we're meant to be together.

JANE   What?

BELLA   MEANT to BE together.

JANE   What makes you say that?

BELLA   I see him everywhere.
          Street corners.
          The bus.
          Sitting on benches in parks.
          Our eyes meet and –
          And SOMETHING happens.

JANE   Yeah?

BELLA   But the thing is.
          We're not ready for each other yet.
          If it happened now it would be all wrong.

JANE   What?

BELLA   All WRONG.

JANE   Right.

BELLA   We're both two restless spirits.
          Searching, questioning –
          But there'll come a point, five years' time maybe,
          when we'll have seen enough, done enough, and
          we'll come face to face, perhaps on a windswept
          heath or on a boat in the middle of the Atlantic, at
          dusk, standing on the deck.

	And it will be –
	Total –
	Recognition.
	Acceptance.
	Empathy.

JANE   Wow.

BELLA   But not yet.
              It's not our time.

JANE   How do you know that?

BELLA   Trust me.
              I know.

              Beat.

              You know your first piece.
              It had sixteen thousand hits.

              Beat.

JANE   Sorry –
              What?

BELLA   You heard me.

JANE   Oh my God.
              Oh my GOD.

BELLA   Happy?

JANE   Happy?
              I'm –
              I can't BELIEVE it!

BELLA   Yeah.
              Well done.

JANE   Shit.
              That means sixteen thousand people read it.
              What.
              WHAT?
              Sixteen thousand people might have HATED it.

BELLA   They didn't.

JANE   Really?

BELLA   Nope.

JANE   Holy CRAP and SAINT JESUS AND MARY!

BELLA   I don't think there is a Saint Jesus.

JANE   I'm FREAKING OUT.

BELLA   So you'd better write another one.
Fast.

JANE   Yeah.

Beat.

Yeah course.

BELLA   You've got ideas.
Right?

JANE   Yeah.
I think so.

BELLA   You think so?

JANE   It's just –
I feel a bit strange now.

BELLA   No.
Don't get all 'Jane' about it.

JANE   What's 'getting all Jane'?

BELLA   Don't feel ashamed just because people are sitting
up and listening.

JANE   Do I do that?

BELLA   This could be something.
I don't plan to write for in-house retail magazines
for ever.

JANE   No I know –

BELLA   Do you want to write press releases for granola
bars for the rest of your life?

JANE   Well.
It's not just granola bars.

	I do yogurt drinks. Sometimes smoothies.
BELLA	You said you had stuff to say.
JANE	I do.
BELLA	So say it. Shout it. This is when it gets fun, Jane! Get in the fucking ring!

Beat.

God I need a pee.
Hold my drink?

Pause.

The BOY *approaches* JANE.

They observe one another.

He smiles.

BOY	You live on my street.
JANE	Do I?
BOY	Yeah. I've seen you.
JANE	Oh. Right.

Pause.

BOY	I work in The Old White Swan.
JANE	I go there.
BOY	I know you do.

Pause.

JANE	I have a boyfriend.
BOY	I know.
JANE	So.

BOY   So?

         Pause.

JANE   We have a cat together.

BOY   He's not here.
         Your boyfriend.

JANE   The cat –
         Isn't doing too well at the moment.

BOY   Whereas I –

JANE   He's listless.

BOY   Am here.

JANE   He isn't eating.

BOY   Standing in front of you.

JANE   His fur is getting dull and his eyes are –
         There's a blankness.

BOY   Do you see what I'm getting at?

JANE   And it's frightening because –
         Because if the cat dies then –
         Then what will be left?
         You know?
         Sorry.
         I'm much drunker than I realised.

         Beat.

BOY   That's one thing you can count on.

JANE   What?

BOY   One day that cat is gonna die.

         Pause.

         Come on.
         Let's go and get a drink.
         Somewhere else.

JANE   Uh.
         I like it here.

BOY	Do you?

BOY   Do you?

JANE   Yeah.

BOY   Why?

Pause.

JANE   I –
Can't.

BOY   Why not?

Pause.

The boyfriend.
The cat.

JANE   No.
My friend she –

BOY   Your friend wouldn't mind.

JANE   No you don't understand she –
Look.

Pause.

JANE   I have responsibilities.
I've made commitments.

BOY   OK.

JANE   And I can't disrupt them.

BOY   Why not?

JANE   Because –
Because those are the rules.

BOY   OK.
I see.

JANE   And when you disregard the rules then –

BOY   Then?

JANE   Then chaos takes hold of you.

BOY   I like chaos.

JANE   Yeah well.
            I don't.

            Pause.

            He smiles.

            He walks away.

            Uh.
            Bye?

BELLA   What were you saying to him?

JANE   Nothing.

BELLA   Did you tell him?
            About me and him and the ship in the Atlantic?

JANE   He wanted to know where the men's was.
            That's all.

BELLA   Oh.
            Why didn't he ask me?

JANE   You weren't here.

BELLA   Why did he leave?

JANE   I think he's a womaniser.

BELLA   That's OK.
            Me and womanisers get along.

JANE   God look at this place.

            They look.

            How old are they all?

BELLA   Dunno.
            Fetuses basically.

JANE   Yeah.

            Pause.

            I looked so great in the mirror at home.

BELLA   Yeah.
            Yeah.

JANE   But I mean –
              Who cares?

BELLA   Well exactly.

JANE   Not me.

BELLA   Not me.

JANE   I'm confident.

BELLA   I'm fucking awesome.

JANE   I mean I've got direction and, and at least I know
              my *place* in the world.
              Right?

BELLA   Right.

              They look.

              We're having a great time.

JANE   Yeah.

BELLA   We're having a better time than them.

JANE   Mm.

BELLA   Right?

JANE   Yeah.
              Right.

              Pause.

              Look I'm going home.

BELLA   Hey.
              What?

JANE   Get home safe, OK.

BELLA   Now?

JANE   That's what I said.

              Beat.

BELLA   Well I'm staying.

JANE   Fine.

BELLA	If I end up raped and decapitated it'll be your fault.
JANE	Get a taxi.
BELLA	Don't leave.
JANE	Have fun. Yeah?
BELLA	Don't leave me. Jane?

Pause.

JANE.

\#

TOBY *and* JANE.

Evening.

JANE	So. So what did the vet say?
TOBY	How was your day?
JANE	It was fine but – What did she say?
TOBY	She said that – Maybe you should sit down.
JANE	Oh God.

Pause.

TOBY	The results from the tests were back and she said – She said that Wilf has got –

Pause.

He's got –
Ha.

It's a –
An Auto-Immune-Deficiency –
Thing.

Pause.

JANE   Right.
            Uh –
            What?

TOBY   An Auto-Immune –
            You *know*.
            You know?

Beat.

JANE   Wilf has got AIDS?

Beat.

TOBY   Don't laugh.

JANE   I'm not, I'm not –

She is.

TOBY   Oh God you're going to set me off now.

JANE   Shit, shit, shit –

TOBY   That's it, laugh it out, laugh it out.

They laugh.

They stop.

*She puts her head in her hands and breathes
deeply.*

Pause.

You OK?

JANE   Yeah.
            No.

TOBY   Yeah.

JANE   Are you OK?

TOBY   Dunno.

JANE   Yeah.

          They breathe.

          God.
          It's –
          What can we do?

TOBY   She said –
          She said there are pills he can take.

JANE   Yeah?

TOBY   But it's more about managing than, than –

          Beat.

JANE   So he's –
          He's not going to –
          Get better.

TOBY   No.

          Beat.

JANE   When?

TOBY   Could be years.

JANE   Oh.

TOBY   Or months.
          Weeks.

JANE   Oh.
          Right.

TOBY   I'm sorry.

JANE   Yeah.
          Me too.

          Pause.

          They put their arms around each other.

          Pause.

TOBY   It's got me thinking though.

JANE   Mm.

TOBY   About –
About you and me.
Our next step.

JANE   What –
What step is that?

TOBY   I feel like –
I really do feel –
That my role in life is to –
Is to be a father.

Silence.

JANE   I see.

TOBY   It's like –
Wilf is our family.
I love our family.

JANE   Yes but.
Wilf is a cat.

TOBY   I want more of it.
Lots more.

JANE   Lots?

TOBY   We could at least talk about it.

Pause.

JANE   We –
We did talk about it.

TOBY   Yes.
And you said we could re-open the discussion in a
year's time and –
And here we are.

Pause.

JANE   I'm not saying I don't want to.
It's worth considering.
It's definitely worth considering.

TOBY   Yes?

JANE   But –
            I'm the one that has to actually –
            Have it.
            Them.

TOBY   Yes.
            I know.
            But –

JANE   And the stuff that happens.
            To your body.

TOBY   Which is kind of amazing.

JANE   And kind of horrible.

TOBY   What's horrible about it?

JANE   The fact that you're never the same.
            Your vagina is never –
            NEVER the same.

TOBY   OK.
            Yes –

JANE   Which you would literally find repulsive.
            By the way.

TOBY   I would not.

JANE   Watching me give birth would make you sick to
            your very soul.
            You'd go running into the streets and leap into
            a taxi.

TOBY   Give me some credit.

JANE   And that's just the beginning.
            Imagine –
            Me.
            Pinned to the sofa by a red, slithery sort of
            otter-thing.
            That's sucking maniacally at my nipple.
            And I'm wild-eyed and keening.

> Hair unbrushed.
> Armpits unshaven.
> Clinging to your legs as you walk out the door
> screaming, 'don't go, don't GO!'

TOBY What if I was the one on the sofa?

JANE What?

TOBY I could do it.
     All of that.

     Beat.

     I mean, obviously not the giving birth bit.

JANE Uh –

TOBY Or the milk, nipple bit.

JANE Well, no –

TOBY But, you know –
     The rest of it!
     You'd keep working.
     I'd stay at home.

     Pause.

     I mean –
     This is the opportunity I've been looking for.
     The most important job of all!
     A father!
     We could be all modern and Scandinavian!

JANE Okeedokee.

TOBY Me and all the other dads in a pavement café.
     Wearing great jumpers.
     Drinking low-alcoholic beers.
     Prams forming a little fortress around us.

JANE Right.

TOBY Making trips to the post office, the butcher's, with
     a sling strapped to my chest.

JANE Right.

TOBY   And then –
         When he's older –

JANE   He?

TOBY   OK then *she* –
         When *she's* older –
         I could take her to the Tate on a Wednesday
         afternoon.
         With a sketchbook.
         She'd have crayons.
         We'd sketch our favourite paintings.

JANE   OK.

TOBY   And at weekends, all three of us could bundle up
         under the covers.
         With the crossword.
         Eating toast in bed.
         Egg and soldiers.
         Getting crumbs in our hair and stuck between
         our toes.

JANE   Well.
         Well who's making the egg and soldiers?

TOBY   Do you realise what I'm saying Jane?

JANE   Me, I bet.

TOBY   What it is I'm offering?

         Pause.

JANE   Yes but.
         It's all very well saying it *in theory* –

TOBY   I'm talking about being The Ultimate Dad!
         Rewriting what Dad means!
         Redefining what *Mum* means most of all!

JANE   But –

TOBY   It's huge, what I'm suggesting –

JANE   Alright.

TOBY   And I'd actually appreciate a little –

JANE   What?

TOBY   Well.
            Acknowledgement.
            At least.

            Pause.

JANE   I don't know.
            It all sounds –
            A bit –
            Dunno.

TOBY   OK.
            Fine.

JANE   What?

TOBY   I can't win.
            Can I?

            Pause.

JANE   You'd be a really good dad.

            Pause.

TOBY   Thank you.

            Pause.

JANE   So.
            There could be a little baby just –
            Right here.

TOBY   Yep.

JANE   Just chilling out.

TOBY   Yep.

JANE   Hiccuping.

TOBY   Maybe.

JANE   Snoring.
            Just gently.

TOBY	Sneezing.
JANE	OK.
	Pause.
	OK I'll think about it.
TOBY	You will?
JANE	Yes.
TOBY	You really will?
JANE	Yes. I really will.
	Beat
	Pass me a beer?

\#

BELLA *and* JANE.

BELLA	These are all the papers that want to interview us.
JANE	Right.
BELLA	How would you feel about going on radio?
JANE	Ummm…
BELLA	OK then I'll do it.
JANE	Oh. Alright.
BELLA	Forty thousand hits last week.
JANE	Whoa.
BELLA	Over a hundred thousand. In the last few days.
JANE	Shit. SHIT.

BELLA	We have haters. Listen – 'You'd better watch out bitch I am coming at you with my giant cock I am going to rip you apart with it and you will like it you fat whore.'
JANE	What?
BELLA	'I will hunt you down and scalp you whilst fucking you from behind with a dildo dykecunt.'
JANE	He said – What?
BELLA	This one's from a woman.
JANE	A woman?
BELLA	'Bitches like u need to learn their place and shut up cos you are talking shit and I am just sick of hearing it so I'm gonna kill your family.'
JANE	God.
BELLA	'You love pussy.' 'You love cock.' 'You love pussy and cock you slut.'
JANE	Uh – Why are you laughing?
BELLA	It's funny.
JANE	Is it?
	Beat.
BELLA	What else can we do?
JANE	I don't know. Cry?
BELLA	This just means it's happening. Jane? It's really happening.
JANE	Yeah.
BELLA	Look happy please.

JANE   All that stuff they're saying.
             It's so –
             Where does that rage come from?

BELLA   People are angry.
             WE'RE angry.

JANE   I know but –
             I feel so –
             Attacked.

BELLA   You can't take it personally.

JANE   I don't want to make people feel that –
             Disgusted.

BELLA   They're the ones who are disgusting, Jane!

JANE   So this doesn't get to you?
             Not at all?

             Beat.

BELLA   You can't let them shame you into crawling away.
             Meek and sorry and afraid.
             Then they'll have won.

JANE   I know.
             But –

BELLA   Of course they hate us!
             What we're saying isn't palatable.
             They feel implicated.

JANE   Maybe –
             I don't know.
             Do you think we're too accusatory?

BELLA   NO.

JANE   OK.

BELLA   Two women a week die at the hands of their
             partners.

JANE   Yes.

BELLA   One in four women will experience domestic
         violence at some point in their lives.
         One in FOUR Jane.

JANE   Yes.

BELLA   Sometimes your boyfriend has sex with you while
         you're fast asleep.

JANE   Uh.
         He does NOT.

BELLA   How do you know?
         You're asleep.

JANE   Because –
         Toby's a good person.
         He'd never –

BELLA   He might.

JANE   He wouldn't.

BELLA   The point is that some people think it's OK.
         Do you think it's OK?
         That Toby's merrily having sex with you left, right
         and centre while you're *fast asleep*?

JANE   HE ISN'T.

BELLA   I think you should write about it.
         That.

JANE   But it doesn't happen –

BELLA   Yes it does.

JANE   Yes but not to me –

BELLA   *So fucking what?*

         Pause.

JANE   You're right.
         You're right.

BELLA   You're allowed to be angry, Jane.
         Even though it isn't pretty.

JANE   Yes.
            I am angry.

BELLA   I know you are.

JANE   We are two furious women.

BELLA   That's right.

JANE   And we're –
            We're really pissing people off.

BELLA   We're getting under their skin.

JANE   We're challenging them.

BELLA   Holding up the mirror.

JANE   And it isn't pleasant.

BELLA   No it is not.

            Beat.

            When are we doing this properly?
            Full-on.
            No excuses.

JANE   What?
            You mean –

BELLA   I feel like the time is right.
            Don't you?
            What do you think?

            Beat.

            We could talk about advertising.
            Potential investors.

            Pause.

JANE   You know I'd want that more than anything.

BELLA   Would you?

JANE   Cos together, it's like we're –
            We're unstoppable.

BELLA   Exactly!

JANE   We make shit happen!

BELLA   Yes!

JANE   But –

BELLA   But?

              Pause.

JANE   I –
              I can't right now.

              Beat.

BELLA   Why not?

JANE   Well.
              Toby he –
              He still doesn't really have a job.
              As such.

              Pause.

BELLA   Oh.

JANE   I'll sort of probably have to pay the rent
              next month.
              All the rent.

BELLA   Oh.

JANE   Which is kind of like –
              YAY feminism.
              Right?

              Pause.

              Me supporting my man!
              Independence!

BELLA   But you're not independent.
              You're depended on.

JANE   But maybe that's a good thing?

              Pause.

BELLA   I just hope that isn't an excuse, that's all.

JANE   What would Toby be excusing?

BELLA   I'm not talking about Toby.

          Pause.

          'Shut your mouth ho no one wanna hear all your
          ranty bullshit 'bout how you hate dick.'

JANE   OK.

BELLA   'No one ever gonna wanna fuck you not if you
          paid me.'

JANE   Alright.

BELLA   'I know where you live I'm coming for you cos
          you made me angry and when I get angry I want
          to rape.'

JANE   Bella –

BELLA   'I'm gonna do it till you die then I'm gonna rape
          your dead body.'

JANE   OK OK I get it.

BELLA   What?

JANE   Can you stop?

BELLA   Write your piece tonight.
          OK?
          We'll put it up tomorrow.
          No excuses, Jane.
          None.

#

JANE *and* TOBY.

TOBY   Wine?

JANE   Oh.
            Thank you.

TOBY   Paintbrush?

JANE   Uh?

TOBY   Hold it a sec.

JANE   OK.
            What's um –
            What's this colour?

TOBY   It's great isn't it?

JANE   Mm.

TOBY   'Squirrel's tail.'

JANE   What?

TOBY   That's what it's called.
            The colour.
            Cool, huh.

JANE   It might be a bit –
            Sludgy.

TOBY   You think?

JANE   Well –

TOBY   Then I'll change it.
            What colour do you want?
            Pick a colour!

JANE   You seem very –
            Happy?

TOBY   I am!
            I feel –
            Alive!
            Awake!

JANE   That's –
         Great.
         How much have you had to drink?

TOBY   I'm here.
         With you!
         I'm painting a wall and I'm drinking wine!
         The world feels full of possibility!

JANE   How's Wilf?

         Beat.

TOBY   Bit sleepy.
         He's on the bed.

JANE   Oh.

TOBY   A bit better.

JANE   Oh good.

TOBY   We had a bit of an altercation over a pill but.
         He took it in the end.

JANE   Oh well done.

TOBY   Chilli's nearly ready.

JANE   You made chilli?

TOBY   Yup.
         Is it too hot in here do you think?

JANE   No it's –
         Perfect.

         Pause.

         JANE *watches him carefully.*

         OK.

TOBY   OK?

JANE   OK.

         She smiles at him.

         They look at each other.

              Let's –
              Do this.

              Pause.

TOBY   Wait –
              You mean?

JANE   Uh-huh.

TOBY   Really?

JANE   Yes.
              Yes.

TOBY   Jane.
              Jane.
              It's a big change.

JANE   Yes.

TOBY   But you feel – ?

JANE   I think so.
              I think so.
              Yes.

TOBY   You honestly feel – ?

JANE   Do you?

TOBY   Yes.
              Yes I do.

              Pause.

TOBY   Wow.
              We're really going to –

JANE   We're really going to.

TOBY   I can't –
              Believe it.

JANE   I know.

              They look at each other.

TOBY   God.
              You're so –
              Beautiful.

JANE   Yeah?

TOBY   Like, this luminous, fertile –
          Goddess.

JANE   Am I?

TOBY   This –
          This earthy, dewy –
          Wanton –
          Gypsy.

JANE   OK.

TOBY   I just want to –

JANE   Yes?

TOBY   Throw you down and –

JANE   And?

TOBY   Defile you.
          Your sparkling, iridescent –
          Womanliness.

JANE   Uh –
          Go on then.
          Defile me.

TOBY   Yes?

JANE   Yes.

TOBY   Yes.

JANE   Yes.
          Yes.
          Yes.

\#

BELLA, JANE, BOY.

Pub.

BELLA	Ohmygod. He's here.
JANE	Who? Oh.
BELLA	Does he work here?
	Beat.
JANE	Looks like it.
BELLA	I'm not going to talk to him.
JANE	Fine.
BELLA	Has he seen me?
JANE	Hard to say.
BELLA	Just act normal OK.
JANE	Fine.
BELLA	So – So guess what?
JANE	What?
BELLA	This is funny.
JANE	OK?
BELLA	So I get a call right. (Is he looking at me?)
JANE	Not right this minute.
BELLA	(What??) So my phone rings and it's this girl. She's called Antonia. She's called Antonia Lovell-Pank.
JANE	Pardon?

BELLA	Exactly. And she's like, hi I'm Antonia Lovell-Pank and I work at *Grazia*.
JANE	*Grazia*?
BELLA	Yup.
JANE	OK.
BELLA	And I'm like, hey Antonia, how you doin'? And she's like, I have Vanessa on the line for you.
JANE	She has Vanessa 'on the line' for you?
BELLA	Yep.
JANE	Because 'Vanessa' can't dial numbers owing to the fact she has no fingers?
BELLA	And then Vanessa pipes up, all perky, and she says – 'What you're doing is very interesting.'
JANE	What?
BELLA	And then she's like. 'You know what Bella? Once upon a time I was just like you. A pioneer.'
JANE	She said you were a pioneer?
BELLA	Then she said I was a maverick.
JANE	Uh-huh.
BELLA	Just like her.
JANE	Wow.
BELLA	So she's like, I think we could work well together. I see so much of myself in you. It's like I'm looking in the mirror. Back to myself, twenty years ago, when I was fresh, and good, and true.
JANE	Shit.

BELLA	And she's like, swing by the office some time. Let's talk. And I'm like – OK I have to think about this.
JANE	You definitely have to think about this. For about five seconds.
BELLA	Yep.
JANE	And then be like – NO.
BELLA	And so she said bye. And I said bye.
JANE	You said bye. For EVER.
BELLA	And then I picked up the phone again and I was like – Sure.

Pause.

JANE	Bella.
BELLA	Just – Listen for a second.
JANE	Bella, no.
BELLA	I know it seems crazy but –
JANE	That's because it IS crazy.
BELLA	I actually think this could be the perfect way to – To really get our voice out there, Jane!
JANE	She'll sink her talons into your flesh and – Contaminate you with all the Botox flowing through her veins.
BELLA	Right at the heart of it. Sucking out the poison!
JANE	She – She gets a blow-dry every single day of her life. And if she can't get her blow-dry, she cries.

BELLA   That's very judgemental.

JANE   She'll befuddle you with praise.
She'll be like, 'Oh wow, we LOVE what you do!
It is SO EDGY!'

BELLA   Maybe it is.

JANE   'You are so totally the VOICE OF A
GENERATION!'

BELLA   Maybe I am.

JANE   Then.
Then she will force you into a scented room and
pin you down and yank out every single one of
your pubic hairs.
And then give you a cupcake.

Pause.

BELLA   You could come too.

Pause.

I'd love you to come with me.

Pause.

JANE   I'm just –
A little confused.
I mean.
Aren't we supposed to despise these Vanessa
people?

Beat.

BELLA   They're just muddling through, same as anyone.
Same as us.

JANE   But –

BELLA   It's not their fault.
Not their fault we're trapped in this bullshit world
where 'a strong woman' equals a babe in a leotard –

JANE   OK –

BELLA   Saying how independent she is whilst eye-fucking
         the camera and caressing her thighs.

JANE   OK I sort of see your point –

BELLA   The problem, let's face it, did not originate with
         Vanessa.

JANE   No but –

BELLA   The problem goes back way, way further than that.

JANE   Yes.
         Yes I see but –

BELLA   And this is a realm where we could make a
         difference!
         You see that right?

JANE   I –
         I don't know.

BELLA   Going right to the nub of it and –
         And making it better!

JANE   You think?

BELLA   Come with me.
         Go on.
         Please.

         Pause.

JANE   I can't.

BELLA   Why not.

JANE   I just –
         They didn't ask me they asked you so –

BELLA   God Jane.

JANE   What?

BELLA   Do you know how you sound sometimes?

         Pause.

I can't tell what you're more scared of.
Failure.
Or success.

Pause.

I'm still waiting for that piece.
Eagerly.

Pause.

I'm going for a pee.

Pause.

JANE *acknowledges the* BOY.

JANE   Why are you always there?

BOY   Nice to see you too.

JANE   Just out of sight but somehow always just –
Here.
Like a cataract.

Pause.

BOY   How's the cat?

Pause.

JANE   He's OK.
Better.

BOY   His soft, furry, pampered life dwindling to nothing?

JANE   No.
He'll be fine.

BOY   We'll see.

JANE   He will.
He has to be.

BOY   Why?

JANE   Because –
Because he's the hook.
The link in the chain.

BOY   Exactly.

          Pause.

JANE   What's the matter with you?
          What have you got against my cat?

BOY   What have you got against your life?

JANE   Who ARE you?

BOY   Who are you?

JANE   That's –
          Don't turn the question around.
          I asked you first.

BOY   I'm serious.
          Who are you?

JANE   Well –
          Why do you care anyway?

BOY   I want to know things about you.
          Is that so bad?

JANE   I don't think that's such a great idea.

BOY   Chaos again?

JANE   It's all getting a bit –
          Churned up.

BOY   Murky.

JANE   Choppy.

BOY   The sharks might rear up and take you in their
          teeth.

JANE   Yes.

BOY   It might all get a bit –
          Bloody.
          Blurry.

JANE   Yes.

BOY	Quite a way to go though. No?

Beat.

BELLA	Hey?
JANE	That was quick.
BELLA	Where'd he go?

Beat.

JANE	Why don't you just go and talk to him?
BELLA	Who?
JANE	Him.
BELLA	Shut UP.
JANE	I'm serious. Why not?
BELLA	God. As if it's that simple.
JANE	Well. It is that simple.
BELLA	Maybe I don't want to be tied down.

Beat.

JANE	By what?
BELLA	By – By the burden of expectation.
JANE	Right.
BELLA	And the inevitable – Rejection.

Beat.

TOBY *waves and approaches.*

Here comes your swain.

JANE   My – ?!
          Oh.
          What's he doing here?

BELLA   You tell me.

TOBY   Sorry to barge in!

JANE   Uh –
          Hi?

TOBY   I can't –
          Sorry –
          I can't find my keys.

JANE   What?

TOBY   Sorry, Bella.

BELLA   It's OK.

JANE   Well just –
          Take mine.

TOBY   Hello.

JANE   Yes, hello – ?

          Pause

TOBY   I think I'll stay for a quick pint actually.
          I'm feeling a bit –
          Flustered.

JANE   But –

TOBY   If I may?

JANE   Well –

BELLA   How's the job-hunt going, Toby?

TOBY   What?

JANE   Bella.

TOBY   Oh what the fuck?
          My wallet?
          I can't find my –
          Oh shit.

JANE   God's sake.
            I'll get you a pint.

TOBY   God, sorry.
            Do you know what?
            I can visualise it on the kitchen table –

JANE   It's *fine*, Toby just –
            Sit down.

            BELLA *and* TOBY *are alone.*

            Silence.

TOBY   So uh –
            How's um…?
            Guy you were…?

BELLA   Who?

TOBY   The guy you were um…?

BELLA   Oh.
            No.

TOBY   Oh?

BELLA   So.

TOBY   Sorry.

BELLA   That's alright.
            Not your fault.

            Silence.

TOBY   So what do you reckon, then?
            Me and Jane?

BELLA   Uh.
            Well you two are –
            Ever delightful.

TOBY   Exciting, isn't it?!

BELLA   I'm not sure that's quite the word I'd –

TOBY   Big step.
            BIG step.

BELLA	Oh?
TOBY	All a bit – 'Crazy'!
BELLA	OK.
TOBY	I mean, Mum thinks we should get married first, yada-yada, but neither of us are really into some kind of expensive, vacuous ceremony, you know?
BELLA	Right.
TOBY	So we thought we'd just – Go for it. I mean – Fuck it!
BELLA	I see.
TOBY	Kids! What the fuck?! Ha!

Beat.

BELLA	Yeah. What the fuck.
JANE	Hurry up and drink this.
TOBY	Uh –
BELLA	No. Don't rush. I'll – Leave you to it.
JANE	Oh don't –
TOBY	I didn't mean to chase you away.
BELLA	Honestly. You two should spend the evening together. Be cosy.
JANE	Bella –

BELLA   It's fine.

             Beat

             I'm meeting her tomorrow at two.
             Sure you won't join me?

             Silence.

             Didn't think so.
             Bye.

             She leaves.

             TOBY *and* JANE *look at each other.*

             Silence.

#

JANE *and* TOBY.

TOBY   There you are.

JANE   Here I am.

TOBY   What you doin'?

JANE   Writing something.
             For the blog.

TOBY   Uh-huh?

JANE   I mean if there even still *is* a blog.
             But –
             Yep.

             Pause.

             You're hovering – ?

TOBY   Oh I was just –
             Thinking about you and me.
             The other night.

JANE   Oh.
         Uh-huh?

TOBY   Wasn't it – ?

JANE   Yep.

TOBY   It really was.

         Pause.

         You're looking particularly –
         Fecund.
         Today.

JANE   Right.

TOBY   Particularly –
         Pregnable.

JANE   Toby.

TOBY   C'mon.
         Just quickly.

JANE   Look I'm –

TOBY   Let's fertilise that little egg.

JANE   Toby –

TOBY   It'll be fun.

JANE   Can you just –

TOBY   The world is ending and it's up to us to repopulate
         the Earth!

JANE   God –

TOBY   It's just the two of us!
         Floating on a sea of devastation!
         The wreckage of a nuclear disaster!

JANE   Um –

TOBY   Our clothes have been burnt to cinders –
         And yet somehow our faces and bodies have
         remained miraculously unblemished!

JANE	Toby – No.
TOBY	We fall upon one another –
JANE	No.
TOBY	With the righteousness of forsaken mankind behind us!
JANE	NO. This is not in ANY WAY erotic to me AT ALL.

Pause.

TOBY	God. Sorry.

Pause.

JANE	Do you even care about what I want? What I might find arousing?
TOBY	Y– Yes.
JANE	Do you?
TOBY	Yes.

Pause.

So.
What?

JANE	What?
TOBY	Tell me.
JANE	Now?
TOBY	Yes.
JANE	You want me to tell you?
TOBY	Yes.
JANE	Honestly?
TOBY	Yes.

Pause.

JANE   OK.

         Pause.

         It shouldn't be this hard.

TOBY   Just –
         Talk.

JANE   You seem quite angry –

TOBY   You wanted to talk.
         So talk.

         Pause.

JANE   I don't –
         I don't want to *talk*.

TOBY   Either you want to talk.
         Or you don't.

JANE   I want –
         I want you to *want* –
         Me.
         Me.

         Pause.

TOBY   I do.

JANE   Not just –
         Not just me as some kind of –
         Vessel.

         Pause.

         I want you to see me.

TOBY   I do.

JANE   No.
         I mean really.
         See me.

         Pause.

TOBY   Do you see me?

JANE   Yes.
          I think so.

          Pause

TOBY   I hope you don't.
          Not really.

          Pause.

JANE   What do you want me to see?

TOBY   I want –
          I want you to see someone who isn't –
          Failing.
          Flailing.

JANE   Are you flailing?

TOBY   I –
          Might be.

JANE   Why?

TOBY   Because I –
          I don't –
          I don't know.

          Beat.

JANE   Come here.

          He hesitates.

          He goes to her.

          They look at each other.

          She kisses him.

          He kisses her back.

          She pulls him to her.

          They sink to their knees.

          They kiss.

          While this is happening, BELLA *is opening up
          her laptop*.

Peering at it.

She takes a deep breath.

BELLA   'SCIENCE *proves* that a woman's ability to conceive DRAMATICALLY decreases after the age of twenty-TWO!'

'People like you is the reason vaginoplasty was invented you fucking bucket.'

'Hey Bella!!!! Gr8 to mt u last week! You got a WIKID body! Things are kinda crazy my end right now so probs can't do it again, soz! Wicked to meet you though, m8!'

JANE *is lying on her back.*

TOBY *is on top of her.*

BELLA *closes her computer.*

TOBY *and* JANE *are kissing.*

BELLA *opens her computer again.*

There is something like horror and something like glee on her face.

'Bella! How fabulous to have you on board at *Grazia*! We're all simply delighted and are certain that you'll be a real asset to the team! Dress code is CASUAL yet TRENDY, FYI.'

'You afraid of the dark? You should be, bitch.'

'SCIENCE proves that men are naturally POLYGAMOUS by nature!!!'

TOBY *and* JANE *look at each other. Smile.*

JANE   Hello.

TOBY   Hello.

They are close and tender.

BELLA   'We had a be-a-yooot-iful baby GIRL and she is GAWWWWGEOUS!!!! Thanks so much peeps we R soooooo blessed!!!'

'You have TWELVE new NOTIFICATIONS!
Could ZANE007 be your LOVE MATCH?!?!?'

'Hey sexy ladie. Wana mt 4 kinkie sex at my
place, I like women be submissive, whipping
very possible.'

BELLA *slams shut her computer.*

TOBY *pulls away from* JANE.

He disentangles himself from her embrace.

Turns away from her.

JANE	What's the matter?
TOBY	Nothing.
JANE	Toby?

Pause.

TOBY	I'm just so – Happy.
JANE	OK.

Pause.

TOBY	This is just everything I want.
JANE	OK. So. Why have you stopped kissing me?

Silence.

TOBY	Shall we make some dinner?
JANE	No.
TOBY	I'm a bit hungry.
JANE	What the *fuck*?
TOBY	What?

They stare at each other.

You like my cooking.

JANE   Why the fuck are we talking about your cooking?

TOBY   OK.
         Chill out.

JANE   The first time we've been remotely close in –
         I don't even know how –

TOBY   That's not true.

JANE   And you're running away.

TOBY   No.
         No I'm just –
         I *told* you.

JANE   This is bullshit.
         If it's not on your fucking terms you just –

TOBY   What?

JANE   Shut down.
         Shut me out.

         Pause.

         Why do you even want a baby with me?

TOBY   What –
         Kind of question is that?

JANE   I want you to answer it.
         Honestly.

         Pause.

         What if there was no baby.
         What then?

TOBY   What –
         What do you mean?

JANE   If it just had to be you and me?

TOBY   Well that's –
         I mean that's irrelevant.

JANE   No.
         I'm asking you.

Just you and me.
What would that mean to you?

TOBY   But –
But the whole point of being in a couple is –
Is to make more of you.
I mean –
That's just the way it is.

Pause.

JANE   Why are you so scared of being on your own?

TOBY   Hang on.
What?

JANE   Why this need to be surrounded?
Safe.

TOBY   That's pretty rich, coming from you.
Ha!

JANE   Why Toby?
Answer me.

Pause.

TOBY   What's wrong with wanting to be safe?

JANE   What's happened to you?

TOBY   Jane?

JANE   You don't even have a job any more.
You just paint and cook and, and fucking *nest*.

TOBY   You love things to be safe!
You practically invented safe!

JANE   I mean what are you?
A fucking *woman*?

Silence.

TOBY   Fuck you.

JANE   Alright.
Fine.

TOBY   You're the one who thinks every man is out to
        fucking –
        Fucking *rape* her.

JANE   Alright, Toby.

TOBY   'Oh it's so HARD for me, I'm so OPPRESSED!'

JANE   You know what, fuck this –

TOBY   'I'm so SCARED to go outside in case one of
        those horrible MEN pulls out a big nasty knife
        and forces me to suck his DICK.'

JANE   Jesus, Toby –

TOBY   And you know what, Jane?
        The irony is –
        No one would FUCKING WANT TO RAPE
        YOU.
        OK?

        Silence.

JANE   That's interesting, Toby.

        Silence.

        Why's that?

        Silence.

        Why would no one want to rape me?

        Silence.

TOBY   I'm sorry.
        That was –
        I'm sorry.

JANE   I'd be really fascinated to hear about it.
        What makes a girl particularly rape-able?

TOBY   That's not what I meant.

JANE   Maybe you'd just like me to keep my mouth shut.
        Bend over.

TOBY   No.

JANE   Put my finger in my mouth and open my eyes
           really, really wide.

TOBY   I'm not that guy.
           You know that.

JANE   Tell you you're the BEST I've ever had.
           You're so STRONG.
           You're so BIG.

TOBY   You know that.

JANE   Please punish me cos I've been SO naughty!

TOBY   What the fuck are you doing?

JANE   Oh pwease don't be angwy wiv lickle old me!

TOBY   Fucking stop it, Jane.

JANE   Tear me apart, you big, powerful LION.

TOBY   Stop it.

JANE   Am I being sexy?
           Is this sexy?

TOBY   What the fuck is your problem?

JANE   Is this turning you on?
           It is, isn't it?
           I can tell.

TOBY   No.
           NO.

JANE   Oh really?
           Really?

TOBY   No, Jane…

JANE   Oh TOBY I want you so badly.

TOBY   No…

JANE   Please Toby.
           Please.

TOBY   Jane stop.

JANE   Please Toby.
              I'm not even fucking kidding just –

TOBY   Stop it... .

JANE   Fucking fuck me.
              Just fucking fuck me.
              Please.
              Now.

#

JANE *and* BELLA.

The train tracks.

BELLA   LOOK AT ME!

JANE   Jesus.
              What are you doing?

BELLA   Are you coming down or what?

JANE   OK.
              Now.
              Slowly.
              Climb back up here OK?

BELLA   Nope.
              Not moving.

JANE   This isn't funny.

BELLA   Not until the very last moment.

JANE   In fact it's stupid.

BELLA   Am I going to have to drag you down here?

JANE   Get off the tracks.

BELLA   With my own bare hands?

JANE   Now.

BELLA   You know what I remembered?
          It was you.
          The one who used to make me do this.
          You.

          Beat.

JANE   I know.

BELLA   You goading and pushing and cajoling and
          bullying.

JANE   Yes.

BELLA   What happened?

          Beat.

JANE   I grew up.

BELLA   You got scared.

JANE   Maybe I did.
          But so did you.

BELLA   So scared that you –
          You decided to opt for the ultimate get-out clause.
          The most convenient excuse not to have to
          commit to anything.
          Ever.

          Pause.

          Toby told me.

          Pause.

          Got a nice, springy bun in the oven yet?

          Pause.

          Congratulations.

JANE   You don't know anything about that.
          Seriously.

BELLA   Look, I'm sorry to be blunt.
          I know I'm being kind of harsh and sorry about
          that –
          But you are so –

JANE   Did you hear what I just said?

BELLA   So cocooned.
          In your muggy, over-decorated little –
          With your CAT.

JANE   You have no idea what is happening in my life.

BELLA   You've made a choice.
          That's cool.

JANE   Because you don't want to know.

BELLA   You've decided to opt out of Fear.
          Of Truth.
          By stuffing wads and wads of loo roll in your ears
          and wrapping yourself in a zillion woolly
          cardigans doused in your boyfriend's aftershave.

JANE   Because you can't admit, even to yourself, that
          you have completely abandoned everything
          you believe in.
          Because you're terrified.

          Pause.

BELLA   Why aren't you down here with me, Jane?

JANE   Because I'm not.

BELLA   Remember how good it used to feel?

JANE   You're not doing it because it feels good.
          You're doing it because you want attention.

BELLA   Remember when you pissed yourself?
          Your mum was so disgusted and you couldn't stop
          laughing –

JANE   'LOOK AT ME!
          TELL ME I'M SPECIAL!
          SLATHER ME WITH PRAISE!'

          Pause.

BELLA   You're the one who's so afraid of putting a foot
          wrong that she never, ever dares to say what
          she really thinks.

JANE   That's not true.

BELLA   Who doesn't even *know* what she really thinks.

JANE   I know I'm sick of this.

BELLA   Get down here, Jane.
        Now.

JANE   No.

BELLA   You wanted to prove yourself.
        So do it.
        Show me.

JANE   I don't have to prove anything to you.

BELLA   SHOW ME.

JANE   You should just trust me.

BELLA   Jane.

JANE   You shouldn't be testing me all the time.

BELLA   There's a train coming.

JANE   I don't have to prove anything to anyone.

BELLA   The tracks.
        They're humming.

JANE   Especially not you.

BELLA   I can't move.

JANE   I don't have to get your approval.
        I don't have to feel afraid of you.

BELLA   I can't move.

JANE   I'm sick of putting everyone else first.
        I'm sick of apologising and second-guessing and
        tiptoeing.
        I'm sick of looking after everyone all the time.

BELLA   Jane I can't move.

JANE   Are you listening to me?
        Is EVERYONE LISTENING TO ME?

BELLA   Something's wrong with me I can't –

JANE   I want you to tell me you hear me.

BELLA   Please.
             Help.

JANE   CAN YOU HEAR ME?

BELLA   Jane PLEASE.

JANE   Bella?
             Bella JUMP.

             The sound of the train.

             JANE *grabs* BELLA*'s hand.*

             They fall on the ground together.

             They breathe.

             They start laughing.

             They laugh for some time.

             Silence.

BELLA   I'm sorry I didn't call you.

JANE   I didn't call you either.

             Pause.

BELLA   I didn't take the job.

             Pause.

             It wasn't for me.

             Pause.

             So.
             What now?

JANE   We keep going.

BELLA   We do?

JANE   We expand.

BELLA   Yes.

JANE   Dive straight into the fire.

BELLA   India.

JANE   Somalia.

BELLA   Uganda.

JANE   We make people listen.

BELLA   We point and scream and wave our arms.

JANE   Cos the minute you start scratching the surface of
            this stuff –
            You either weep or –

BELLA   Or you go to battle.

            Pause.

JANE   You should go.
            Be our foreign correspondent.

BELLA   But not you?

JANE   You'd be good at it.

            Pause.

            'The Girl's Guide to Saving the World'
            At home and abroad.

BELLA   That could work.

            Pause.

            If someone told you you were going to be alone
            for the rest of your life.
            How would you feel about it?

JANE   I don't know.

            Pause.

            OK, I guess.

BELLA   Yeah.
            It's not that bad, is it?

JANE   It's not that bad.

            Pause.

BELLA   Come on.
           Let's get out of here.

JANE   I think I'll stay.
           For a bit.

BELLA   OK.

JANE   Bella?

           Beat.

BELLA   It was fun wasn't it?

JANE   Yeah.
           It was.

#

BELLA, MAN.

A bus stop.

MAN   Hey.
           I know you don't I?

           Silence.

           Hey?
           I'm TALKING to you.

BELLA   Yeah?

           Pause.

           What is it you want to say, exactly?

           Pause.

           Tell me what beautiful eyes I have?
           Ask me what I'm doing alone on such a dark night?
           Show me your cock?

           Pause.

>That's right.
>Sometimes we speak.
>
>*Pause*.
>
>Fucking prick.

#

JANE, WOMAN.

WOMAN   Jane, yes?

JANE   That's right.

WOMAN   Have you got your knickers off for me?

JANE   Yes.

>*Pause*.

WOMAN   Now I need you to bend your legs up –
Good.
And now let them flop open.
OK.
That's fine.
Now this next bit might feel a bit cold –

>JANE *gasps*.
>
>That's it.
>
>*Pause*.

JANE   Is it going to –
Hurt?
I mean the actual –
Thing.

WOMAN   I'm about to give you an injection to numb
the cervix.
That should prevent any pain.

JANE   Right.

WOMAN   Some people feel mild discomfort.

JANE   Uh-huh.

            Pause.

            And it takes –
            How long?

WOMAN   We'll be all done in ten minutes.

JANE   Oh.
            Great.

WOMAN   Is someone picking you up?

JANE   No.
            Just me.

WOMAN   OK.

            Pause.

            You might feel a bit light-headed afterwards.
            Make sure you're ready to leave.

JANE   I have to drink the tea.
            I know.

            Pause.

WOMAN   OK.
            If you could just try and relax for me.
            That's it –

JANE   Can it feel anything?

            Pause.

WOMAN   The fetus won't feel any pain.

JANE   Are you sure?

WOMAN   It's very early.

JANE   OK.
            OK.

            Pause.

WOMAN   Right, now you'll feel a short sharp scratch –

JANE   Wait.

WOMAN   Sorry?

          Pause.

          Do you want me to carry on?

JANE   I uh –

WOMAN   I can stop if you're –

JANE   No.
          I'm.

          Pause.

          I'm sure.

WOMAN   This is what you want?

JANE   Yes.
          This is what I want.

          Pause.

WOMAN   Shall we try again?

JANE   Yes.
          Yes I'm ready.

\#

JANE *and* TOBY.

Silence.

TOBY He's throwing up a lot.

JANE Oh.

TOBY Mum keeps finding him in the airing cupboard.

JANE Yeah?

TOBY All her sheets are covered in white hairs.

   Silence.

   He's not very happy.

JANE No.

TOBY He's not very happy…

   Silence.

   Although sometimes he's alright.
   I pick him up and –
   He's so light now, you can pick him up with
   one hand –
   And I take him into my room and I make a sort
   of den for him out of old T-shirts.
   I think he likes the smell.
   The past.

JANE Yeah.

TOBY And he sort of hunkers down and tucks himself up
   really small and he purrs.
   Really quietly.

   Pause.

   So sometimes I think he might be OK.

   Pause.

JANE I think it's probably time, Toby.

   Pause.

TOBY   He has a nice life.
          He potters around in the garden.
          Eats salmon.

JANE   I know.

TOBY   Or sniffs salmon.
          He doesn't actually –
          I mean he sort of –
          Can't really eat at the moment.

JANE   Yes.

TOBY   But it could just be a phase.
          There are these anti-nausea pills that are really
          amazing and –

JANE   Toby –

TOBY   It could just be a phase.

JANE   OK.

TOBY   Couldn't it?

          Silence.

JANE   I'll come down and –
          And we'll go together.

          Silence.

TOBY   Being the one who makes that choice I can't –
          I mean –
          Why should we be the ones who get to decide?

JANE   We're doing it for him.

TOBY   Are we?

JANE   Yes.
          Yes.

          Pause.

TOBY   So, what?
          We put him in his carrier-thing and we put it in the

car and we drive the car to the vet's and we just –
That's what we do?

Pause.

JANE   Yes.

TOBY   I can't.

JANE   Yes you can.
We have to.

Pause.

TOBY   I know you're right.
But.

JANE   I know.

Pause.

TOBY   I'll phone them.
This afternoon.

JANE   OK.

TOBY   I could –
Stick around?

Silence.

JANE   Let me know when and –
And I'll come up.

Silence.

TOBY   I sort of thought he'd live for ever.

JANE   I know.
Me too.

Pause.

TOBY   Are you sure, Jane?
Are you *sure*?

JANE   I am.

TOBY   There's no other way?
No other option?

JANE   No.

TOBY   Because if there is –

           Pause.

           But there isn't.
           I know that.

#

JANE *and the* BOY.

JANE   You were right.

BOY   What?

JANE   The cat.
           He died.

           Pause.

           Have you ever had the realisation –
           That you are completely on your own?

BOY   Now that's the whisky talking –

JANE   This is me.
           Talking.

           Beat.

           Once you realise it.
           It's horrifying at first.
           But then you realise that it makes you utterly –
           Free.

BOY   Yes.

JANE   To do all the things you want.
           And these things.
           They might not be good.
           They might be bad.

> Hurtful.
> Destructive.
>
> *Pause.*
>
> I could reach over and touch you.

BOY   You could.

JANE   You're there.

BOY   I am.

JANE   And I'm.
Here.

BOY   Yes.

JANE   I like that.

BOY   Yeah?

JANE   Yes.

Pause.

I'd like to stand next to you at a party.
Surrounded by people.
And feel your fingers on my lower back.
And I'd know.
I'd know what you wanted to do.

BOY   What would I want to do?

JANE   You'd want to press my back a little harder.
Push me.
Guide me through the people.
You'd be smiling and nodding to everyone.
They wouldn't be able to tell that you had your
hand on my back.
The urgency of it, propelling me forward.

BOY   Then what?

JANE   We'd start climbing a staircase.
Hundreds and hundreds and hundreds of stairs.
I'd be wearing a yellow dress.

Hundreds and hundreds and hundreds of layers.
Your hand would still be on my back.
I wouldn't turn round.
Not once.
Not until we reached the top.
There'd be a tiny room, in a turret.
It would smell of jasmine.
You'd walk over to the window, open it.
A peacock would fly past, its feathers brushing
my face.
We'd climb out the window, onto the roof.
Gently you'd push me down onto the tiles, the
yellow dress fanning out around me.
You'd bend down, as if you were going to kiss me,
and everything in me would hold its breath.
But then you wouldn't.
You'd keep me waiting.
And waiting.
And waiting.
Because you'd know that it's the waiting that's the
best bit.
When it's all in the future.
The sweat, the skin, the hair, the flesh, the bone.
It's that moment.
That's the moment I want.

Pause.

BOY   So come upstairs.

Pause.

JANE   No.

BOY   Why not?

JANE   Because you're just a fantasy.

BOY   Is that so bad?

Pause.

Go on then.
Do what you have to do.
You'll live.

JANE	Don't worry.
	I know.

	The End.

A Nick Hern Book

The Girl's Guide to Saving the World first published in Great Britain in 2014 as a paperback original by Nick Hern Books Limited, The Glasshouse, 49a Goldhawk Road, London W12 8QP, in association with HighTide Festival Theatre

The Girl's Guide to Saving the World copyright © 2014 Elinor Cook

Elinor Cook has asserted her right to be identified as the author of this work

Cover image: 'Explosions in the Sky' by Aneta Ivanova (www.anetaivanova.com)

Designed and typeset by Nick Hern Books, London
Printed in Great Britain by Mimeo Ltd, Huntingdon, Cambridgeshire PE29 6XX

A CIP catalogue record for this book is available from the British Library

ISBN 978 1 84842 389 3

CAUTION   All rights whatsoever in this translation are strictly reserved. Requests to reproduce the text in whole or in part should be addressed to the publisher.

Amateur Performing Rights   Applications for performance, including readings and excerpts, by amateurs in the English language throughout the world should be addressed to the Performing Rights Manager, Nick Hern Books, The Glasshouse, 49a Goldhawk Road, London W12 8QP, *tel* +44 (0)20 8749 4953, *e-mail* info@nickhernbooks.co.uk, except as follows:

Australia: Dominie Drama, 8 Cross Street, Brookvale 2100, *tel* (2) 9938 8686 *fax* (2) 9938 8695, *e-mail* drama@dominie.com.au

New Zealand: Play Bureau, PO Box 9013, St Clair, Dunedin 9047, *tel* (3) 455 9959, *e-mail* play.bureau.nz@xtra.co.nzz

South Africa: DALRO (pty) Ltd, PO Box 31627, 2017 Braamfontein, *tel* (11) 712 8000, *fax* (11) 403 9094, *e-mail* theatricals@dalro.co.za

United States of America and Canada: The Agency (London) Ltd, see details below

Professional Performing Rights   Applications for performance by professionals in any medium and in any language throughout the world (and amateur and stock performances in the United States of America and Canada) should be addressed to The Agency (London) Ltd, 24 Pottery Lane, Holland Park, London W11 4LZ, *fax* +44 (0)20 7727 9037, *e-mail* info@theagency.co.uk

No performance of any kind may be given unless a licence has been obtained. Applications should be made before rehearsals begin. Publication of this play does not necessarily indicate its availability for amateur performance.